The
Power
of
Expectation

David M. Blunt

THE POWER OF EXPECTATION
by David M. Blunt
ISBN 1-893716-05-08

Published by
Executive Books
206 West Allen Street
Mechanicsburg, PA 17055

Toll-free: 800-233-2665
In PA: 717-766-9499
Fax: 717-766-6565

Visit our website: www.executivebooks.com

Table of Contents

Dedication

To my wife, Kim,
and my two sons, Daniel and Stephen.
To God be the glory!

CHAPTER 1

What Are You Expecting?

God meets us at the level of our expectation. He doesn't meet us according to our personality. He doesn't meet us according to our degree of talent and ability. He doesn't meet us according to our financial condition. He doesn't meet us according to our educational background. He doesn't meet us according to our age or marital status. He doesn't meet us according to the color of our skin. He meets us according to our level of expectation.

What does that mean? It means that God can only do for us what we *believe* He can do for us. It means that if we can expand and enlarge and increase our level of expectation, we can expand and enlarge and increase what God can do in our lives.

Our level of expectation sets the limits for our life. It determines how much God can accomplish in us, through us, and for us. If we only expect little, God is only able to do little. But if we expect much, God is able to do much.

7

We can literally change our world by changing the level of our expectation.

God is able and willing to work in our lives, and He has every intention of doing so.

PHILIPPIANS 1:6 (NIV)

> 6 *Being confident of this, that he who began a good work in you will carry it on to completion until the day of Christ Jesus.*

Hebrews 12:2 calls Jesus "the author and finisher" of our faith. His desire is to bring to completion everything He has ever birthed in our heart.

And no one can stop Him. No one has the power to stop God from carrying out His plan for your life. Not your friends. Not your family. Not your foes. Not your in-laws. Not your outlaws. Not your spouse. Not your children. Not the world. Not the government. Not your teachers. Not office politics. Not even the devil. No one can stop God's plan for you. No one.

God meets us at the level of our expectation.

Except you. You and your level of expectation. If you think little, believe little, pray little, and expect little, you will receive little, even though God Himself is personally ready and willing to move on your behalf. *You* can limit what He is able to do in your life.

The good news is that you don't have to settle for little. If you don't like your world, you can change it. If you'll start thinking big, believing big, praying big, and expecting big, you'll start receiving big. That's a fact.

So the question for you today is, what are you expecting? Are you expecting God to do little or are you expecting God to do much? Your answer is important. Your future depends on it.

CHAPTER 2

Expectation Is An Inside Job

*I*f we really want to see God begin to do big things in our life, we *must* make sure that our "expector" is in good working condition. In order to do that, we need to understand some things.

First of all, the kind of expectation we're talking about isn't based on external events or circumstances. It's an inside job.

We have expectations about a lot of different things in life. Expectations about a new car. Expectations about a new house. Expectations about a raise on our job. Expectations about a vacation we're planning to take. We even have expectations about what we want for Christmas!

But guess what? Things don't always turn out the way we expect. We don't always get what we want for Christmas. (After all, you may have been a very bad little boy all year long!) We may end up getting that tie that we never, ever wanted instead of what we really had in mind.

If our expectations are based on events or circumstances, we're headed for disappointment. Oh, we'll be in a good mood and have a positive attitude as long as the circumstances are favorable. We'll have high expectations and be excited as long as we have a special event to look forward to. But what about the rest of the time? What about when circumstances *aren't* so favorable? What about when we *don't* have a particular event to look forward to?

If our expectations are based on events or circumstances, we're headed for disappointment.

If we really want to see God begin to work in our life, we have to raise our level of thinking. Life is more than getting up, going to work, coming home, and going on vacation once a year. Life is more than accumulating more stuff. Life is more than what people do or don't do. Life is more than what is going on in our present circumstances. We have to expand our thinking and our expectations beyond that level.

The kind of expectation we're talking about goes beyond events and circumstances. It's not rooted in those things. It's rooted in God. It's a supernatural force that comes from having faith in God and His Word. It comes from the inside out.

Because the God-kind of expectation is not based on natural things, it never becomes discouraged. It keeps on expecting, even when there are delays and disappointments. It keeps on expecting, even when the situation looks impossible. It keeps on keeping on.

The Bible tells us in Romans 4 that Abraham had this kind of expectation.

ROMANS 4:18 (AMP)

18 *[For Abraham, human reason for] hope being gone, hoped in faith that he should become the father of many nations, as he had been promised "So [numberless] shall your descendants be."*

The Bible says that in the natural realm, Abraham didn't have any reason at all to have hope. The situation truly looked impossible. But Abraham's expectations weren't based on the natural realm. They were based on God's promise. And because they were based on God's promise, Abraham hoped on anyway, regardless of what things looked like.

When the world talks about hope, it's really just talking about desire. There's no certainty about it. There's no confidence about it. It's a term full of doubt and unbelief. It's simply a matter of wishful thinking.

But Bible hope is different. In the New Testament, the word *hope* actually means "to expect" or "expectation." (In the Old Testament, the word *wait* often means the same thing.) Unlike the world's definition of hope, the Bible definition is full of certainty. It is the confident assurance that what God has promised will come to pass in your life. That's Bible hope.

Going back to Abraham for just a moment, we see that this is exactly the kind of hope he had.

ROMANS 4:20-21 (AMP)

20 *No unbelief or distrust made him waver (doubtingly question) concerning the promise of God, but he grew strong and was empowered by faith as he gave praise and glory to God,*

21 *Fully satisfied and assured that God was able and mighty to keep His word and to do what He had promised.*

We can't say it any better than that. Bible hope is being confident that God means what He says and then fully expecting Him to do what He has promised.

My wife and I began pastoring our present church in 1983. Just for the record, there have been some discouraging times along the way. Some people have let us down. There have been delays and disappointments with various projects. But we're still here. We never lost hope. We never lost our expectation that God would do what He had promised us.

I remember those early days when we started with only 35 people. I remember telling our Music Department (which at that time was only two or three people singing some songs) that we were going to have an orchestra and a choir with robes.

Now at that time, it wasn't popular to have a choir with robes in a charismatic church. It wasn't being done. You wouldn't believe the insult and criticism I was subjected to just to birth a choir with robes!

~~But~~ I really didn't care what everybody else was doing. I wasn't doing this because somebody else was doing it. I had a dream from God down on the inside! It didn't matter what people said. It didn't matter what things looked like. I had hope! I expected God to do what He said. And guess what? Today our charismatic church has an orchestra—*and* a choir with robes. Glory to God!

Abraham's expectations weren't based on the natural realm.

In the early days of our church, we met in a rented 4,000-square-foot building. We all met in one big room—nursery, children's ministry, choir, everybody. One room. We had a soundboard from Radio Shack that crackled and whistled and did all kinds of strange things. (I think it was demon-possessed!) We certainly didn't look very successful at that point in time. But I had expectations!

Eventually we began looking for land. Initially, I wanted something right off of the interstate, but God had a better plan.

When He opened up some other property for us and we began moving in that direction, not everyone thought it was a good idea. "You'll never make it out there! That's too far out in the country. It'll never happen there!" I came under all kinds of criticism for that. But I had hope! I expected God to do what He said.

Bible expectation isn't moved by how we feel or what things look like.

And guess what? It *is* happening out here! Today we average 4,000 people in attendance each weekend. We give over $1 million to missions each year. We have over 20 acres on our campus and we are totally debt free as a ministry. Glory to God!

What kept me going when the doubters and pouters were against me? Expectation. Expectation down on the inside of me. It's a powerful force.

Oral Roberts popularized the expression "Something good is going to happen to you." That's Bible hope. That's Bible expectation. It's the conviction that the good things

God has put in your heart will come to pass. That's what kept me going. That's what carried me through to victory.

Never let go of your expectation. Even if no one else seems to be on your side, *you* keep expecting.

HEBREWS 10:23 (NKJV)

23 *Let us hold fast the confession of our hope without wavering, for He who promised is faithful.*

Speak your expectation, not what you're experiencing. It doesn't matter what things look like. It doesn't matter what anyone else says. It only matters what God says—and what *you* say in response to Him. Hold onto your expectation! God is faithful!

Bible expectation comes with endurance. When we have high expectations about tomorrow, then we'll have the endurance to wait until tomorrow. And if our answer doesn't manifest tomorrow, then we'll have the endurance to wait until the next day and the next. We won't give up just because things didn't go quite right today. We won't give up today, because even though we have no idea what God is going to do in our life tomorrow, we know that it will be exceedingly, abundantly above all that we can ask or think. It will be worth showing up for. It will be worth waiting for because God will be there.

If we're going to make it in life, our expectations can't be built upon external things. They have to be built on an internal relationship with God. If my expectation comes from my job, what happens when I lose my job? I lose my expectation. If my expectation is based on receiving a Christmas bonus, what happens if I don't receive a Christmas bonus? I lose my expectation. But if my expectation comes from God, then anything can happen on the outside and it won't stop me from expecting on the inside.

Speak your expectation, not what you're experiencing.

I'll just keep on keeping on, because my expectation is rooted in God.

Bible expectation can't be defeated by events and circumstances. Bible expectation isn't moved by what people say or how they treat us. Bible expectation isn't moved by whether or not we are overlooked for that promotion. Bible expectation isn't moved by whether or not we receive a bad report from the doctor. Bible expectation isn't moved by how we feel or by what things look like. Delays can't distract it. Disappointments can't overcome it. Discouragement can't defeat it. It's rooted in God. It's an inside job.

CHAPTER 3

The Benefits Of Expectation

*T*he second thing we need to understand about expectation is that it provides us with benefits—benefits which give us the strength we need to live a victorious life.

PSALM 31:24 (AMP)
24 *Be strong and let your heart take courage, all*
you who wait for and hope for and expect the Lord!

Basing our hope and expectation in God produces strength. Not just PMA (positive mental attitude) or wishful thinking. Not just something that lasts for the moment. Something powerful. Something real. Something you can take to work with you. Something you can take to school with you. A strength and courage that are able to carry you through *anything* you will ever have to face in this life.

People who are depressed, people who want to commit suicide, are people who have no sense of expectation from God. How can we say that? We see it in God's Word.

The Word of God provides us with clear evidence that expectation enables us to endure whatever comes our way without wavering.

HEBREWS 12:2

2 *Looking unto Jesus the author and finisher of our faith; who for the joy that was set before him endured the cross, despising the shame, and is set down at the right hand of the throne of God.*

Jesus had a sense of expectation about His life. He believed that God was going to do what He had promised. That's what gave Him strength to endure the cross. That's what kept Him from despairing. That's what kept Him from throwing in the towel and quitting.

Bible expectation. It produces the vitality and energy we need to keep pressing on, even when things are difficult. It produces the courage we need to take risks and do what we've never done before. It produces the stamina we need to remain steady in the midst of turmoil. Without it, we'll never endure in this life.

Faith Produces Expectation

What are the benefits of expectation and how do they bring about victory in our life? Let's picture it as a process—a process that begins with faith.

The Bible gives us a simple definition of faith in Hebrews 11.

HEBREWS 11:1
1 *Now faith is the substance of things hoped for, the evidence of things not seen.*

Faith is the assurance in our heart that what we're expecting is true. Faith is what gives substance to our God-given expectations and enables them to come to pass. The *Amplified Bible* says it this way:

HEBREWS 11:1 (AMP)
1 *Now faith is the assurance (the confirmation, the title deed) of the things [we] hope for, being the proof of things [we] do not see and the conviction of their reality [faith perceiving as real fact what is not revealed to the senses].*

Faith is the assurance that the fulfillment of God's promises is a fact, regardless of what things looks like.

As far as faith is concerned, the promises of God are a "done deal." It doesn't matter if you can't see them yet. It doesn't matter if you can't touch them yet. You just know they're true. Faith is the title deed that says they're yours.

Faith, that inner confidence and assurance, is the proof of those things you can't see. If you could see them, you wouldn't need faith. You'd have other evidence. If you could touch them, you wouldn't need faith. You'd have other evidence. But in this area of spiritual realities which haven't manifested yet, you *do* need faith. In this case, *faith* is your evidence. *Faith* is your proof. But it's the only proof you need.

Because faith is based on the promises of God, no other evidence is necessary. You know it's yours because God said so. Period. Case closed. And that kind of faith sends your expectation level soaring!

If we're not expecting, we're not in faith.

Faith produces expectation. If we're not expecting, we're not in faith. The two go hand in hand. Faith is the confident assurance that the promises of God are real and that they belong to us. Expectation is the confident assurance that God will bring those promises to pass in our life. The two work together. When we're walking in faith, we'll also be walking in expectation.

Are you expecting God's promises to come to pass in your life today? If you are, then you're in faith. But if you're in the "Whatever will be, will be" mentality, you're not in faith. The evidence of faith is confident expectation. A day without expectation is a day without faith. If you get up on Monday morning, just planning to endure the day, just planning to get through the day, not expecting God to do anything in your life, then that's a day of doubt and unbelief for you. But if you get up expecting God to do exceedingly, abundantly above all that you can ask or think, then that's a day of faith for you.

Faith honors God. It pleases Him. In fact, Hebrews 11:6 goes so far as to say that we can't please God without it.

HEBREWS 11:6
6 *But without faith it is impossible to please him: for he that cometh to God must believe that he is, and that he is a rewarder of them that diligently seek him.*

So then if faith produces expectation, and expectation is evidence of our faith, we could also say that we can't please God without expectation. It honors Him when believe that He is God and when we expect that He is going to perform His Word in our life.

Expectation Produces Joy

And what's the fruit of that expectation? Joy. Faith produces expectation and expectation produces joy. Besides telling us that we must have faith to please God, note that Hebrews 11:6 also tells us that He is a rewarder. Our expectations aren't just wishful thinking. They're going to result in answers from God!

What greater joy than to know that we are in right relationship with God, that we are pleasing to Him, and that He is working on our behalf to see that His Word comes to pass in our life! That's real joy. It doesn't come from people. It doesn't come from events or circumstances. It's an inside job, just like expectation. It's rooted in God.

So faith produces expectation and expectation produces joy. I Peter 1:8 says it another way.

I Peter 1:8
8 *Whom having not seen, ye love; in whom, though now ye see him not, yet believing, ye rejoice with joy unspeakable and full of glory. . . .*

Believing produces rejoicing. If we're not rejoicing, then we're not believing. If we'll get back to believing, then we'll get back to rejoicing. The two go together.

24

Believing is a choice—which means rejoicing is a choice. Nobody can stop our believing without our permission. And no one can stop our rejoicing without our permission. If we let stuff be the source of our believing and rejoicing, then when our stuff is taken away, we'll lose our rejoicing. But if we let our believing and rejoicing be rooted in God, then nothing can destroy it. If we'll start believing, then we can rejoice in the midst of anything—disappointment, discouragement, delay, offenses, hurt, pain, problems, suffering, anything—because we're expecting God to do what He said He would do.

If we'll put our faith and expectation in God and His Word, we'll get to the point where nothing moves us—except Him. Philippians tells us that Paul was that way.

PHILIPPIANS 4:11-12 (AMP)

11 . . . *for I have learned how to be content (satisfied to the point where I am not disturbed or disquieted) in whatever state I am.*

12 *I know how to be abased and live humbly in straightened circumstances, and I know also how to enjoy plenty and live in abundance. I have learned in any and all circumstances the secret of facing every situation, whether well-fed or going hungry, having a sufficiency and enough to spare or going without and being in want.*

It didn't matter what people said to him. It didn't matter what people did to him. It didn't matter what was going on around him. Paul's faith and expectation were in God, not people or circumstances. And because of that, he never lost his joy. The world didn't give it to him and the world couldn't take it away.

My wife and I learned that lesson when we were in Bible college. Sometimes I've heard people complain that they were having such problems that they didn't even have a turkey for Thanksgiving. Well, neither did we, but we decided not to let that turkey keep us from being eagles!

Believing produces rejoicing.

On Thanksgiving of 1976, we were away from home at Bible college in Minneapolis, Minnesota. Kim was working full-time. I was working part-time and going to college full-time. We wanted to go home, but we couldn't do that because we didn't have money for gas. We wanted to have a traditional turkey dinner with all the trimmings, but we couldn't do that because we didn't have money for a traditional turkey dinner. But we decided to rejoice and have Thanksgiving dinner anyway! We literally put our pennies and nickels together, went down to the grocery store, and bought a Totino's frozen pizza. (To give you an idea of how little money we're talking about, I just saw that same pizza on sale the other day for 79 cents!) It wasn't a traditional turkey dinner, but that didn't matter. It was dinner! So we rejoiced, with confident expectation that God was working in our lives and that brighter days were ahead for us.

If we're in faith and we're in expectation, we'll have joy. It won't matter what we have for Thanksgiving dinner. We'll be able to eat Totino's frozen pizza and rejoice because God has given us expectations for our future. It won't matter what's under the Christmas tree, because we know Who was on "the tree"—Jesus! And because of what He accomplished on that tree (the cross), all of the promises of God are now available to us.

II CORINTHIANS 1:20 (NIV)

20 *For no matter how many promises God has made, they are "Yes" in Christ. And so through him the "Amen" is spoken by us to the glory of God.*

Exercising our faith is how we say "Amen" to the promises of God. The word *amen* means "so be it." When we exercise our faith, we're giving God the OK to work in our life. We're releasing Him to do what He has already promised to do for us. Once we do that, it's just a matter of time before we see the fulfillment of the promise. Now that's something to rejoice about!

Which would you rather have, one fish or a fishing company? If you're just looking for one fish, your expectation level isn't very high. Your joy isn't going to last very long. When that one fish is gone, there goes your expectation. There goes your joy. It all ends there. But if you have a fishing company, the possibilities are limitless. There is an endless supply of fish available to you.

If we're basing our expectation and joy on a particular person or organization or event, we're settling for just one fish. But God wants us to expand and increase and enlarge our level of expectation so that He can expand and increase and enlarge our level of joy. If we'll expect big things from Him, He'll give us the wisdom to own the fishing company so that we can enjoy an endless supply of blessing from Him, regardless of our circumstances. Even when we can't see or touch the answer, we'll rejoice in the confidence that it is on the way!

Joy Produces Strength

That kind of joy—inside joy, joy from the Lord—is what produces strength.

NEHEMIAH 8:10

10 *. . . the joy of the LORD is your strength.*

Nothing lifts you and encourages you like knowing that God is on your side and actively working on your behalf.

Joy is the result of our expectations. Our expectations are the result of our faith in God and His Word. If we don't have any strength today, it's because we don't have any joy. And if we don't have any joy, it's because we're not expecting God to do anything in our life.

"Well, Pastor, I think life's a drag. I'm always getting beat up. I always seem to be going around in circles, never getting ahead. I always feel left out and behind everybody else. All I ever seem to end up with is Murphy's Law. I don't really expect much to happen in my life because he did this and she did that and the church did that and. . . ." When we talk like that, we're saying that we have no faith in God and His Word.

Hope for the future gives us power for the present.

If that's how you've been thinking, it's time to change channels. It's time to raise your level of expectation. If you don't, you'll never have any joy. And without joy, you won't have any strength.

Our expectations about our future in God give us a joy that empowers us to do what we need to do today. We saw earlier in Hebrews 12:2 that Jesus was able to endure the cross because of "the joy that was set before Him." Hope for the future gives us power for the present.

So it's important to know that God has plans for your life—good plans—and it's time for you to tap into them.

JEREMIAH 29:11 (NIV)
11 *"For I know the plans I have for you," declares the LORD, "plans to prosper you and not to harm you, plans to give you hope and a future."*

God's the One Who gives us hope. He's the One Who gives us a future. If you'll hook up with Him and His Word, you'll always have plenty to hope for. You'll always be full of expectation. You'll fully expect that tomorrow will be better than today. You'll fully expect that this year will be better than last year. You'll fully expect that what He has promised will come to pass in your future. And the joy that results from those expectations will give you the strength you need to arrive there.

God created us to be winners, not whiners. He wants us to make progress in life. He wants us to achieve. He wants us to advance. He wants us to go forward. How do we do that? By having joy in our faith.

PHILIPPIANS 1:25 (NIV)
25 . . . and I will continue with all of you for your progress and joy in the faith.

Paul said that progress and the joy of faith go together. We can't make progress without joy. And we can't have joy without faith. No faith, no joy. No joy, no progress. Faith produces expectation, expectation produces joy, and joy gives us the strength we need to make progress.

We saw in Philippians 4:11-12 that Paul knew how to walk in the joy of the Lord. The next verse goes on to explain how that joy energized and empowered him to meet every challenge of life successfully.

PHILIPPIANS 4:13 (AMP)
13 I have strength for all things in Christ Who empowers me [I am ready for anything and equal to anything through Him Who infuses inner strength into me; I am self-sufficient in Christ's sufficiency.]

Wow! What an incredible statement! When you've got God, you've got everything you need. Faith. Hope. Joy. Confidence. Strength. Endurance. Stamina. A future.

Strength Produces Victory

Victory. That's what we're all after, isn't it? Victory in our finances. Victory in our marriages. Victory in our families. Victory in our jobs. Victory in our callings. Victory in our relationships. Victory in our health. Victory over our future. Victory in every circumstance we face. We want to be up in a down world. We want to be victors, not victims.

How do we get to be victors? By faith. The Bible says it's faith that makes us overcomers.

I JOHN 5:4
4 *For whatsoever is born of God overcometh the world: and this is the victory that overcometh the world, even our faith.*

When we walk in faith, we walk in victory.

How does that happen? How do we progress from faith to victory?

- Faith produces expectation.
- Expectation produces joy.
- Joy produces strength.
- Strength produces victory.

The power of expectation makes us winners every time!

CHAPTER 4

Check Your Gauges

*I*f we want to make sure we're headed in the right direction, it's important to know where we are now. Although God has promised us victory, the devil is going to do everything he can to throw us off course. To be sure that we're staying on track, we need to continually check up on ourselves and make any necessary adjustments.

We've already seen that if we expect to walk in victory, we have to be walking in faith. But how do we know if we're doing that?

ROMANS 15:13

13 *Now the God of hope fill you with all joy and peace in believing, that ye may abound in hope, through the power of the Holy Ghost.*

Joy, peace, and hope (or expectation). Those are the checkpoints. Those are the things we need to see in our life.

The verse says that if we're believing (or we're in faith), we'll have joy and peace and be abounding in hope (expectation). That's pretty easy to check, isn't it? If I'm walking around feeling sorry for myself, I'm not in faith. If I'm looking around at what other people have and then getting depressed because I don't have as much, I'm not in faith. If I'm always confused and frustrated, I'm not in faith. If I'm convinced that no matter what I do, things will never get better for me, then I'm not in faith.

If we're in doubt, we'll be without.

Joy, peace, and expectation. If I have them, I'm in faith. If I don't have them, I'm not in faith. It's that simple.

If our journey in life is going to be a victorious one, those three tanks have to stay full as we travel down the road to victory in our Christianmobile. We have to keep an eye on those gauges. That's how we stay on the faith road. That's how we stay on the victory road.

We have to keep an eye on that joy gauge. Are we able to rejoice, even when things don't seem to be going right? If not, then it's time to fill up.

We have to keep an eye on that peace gauge. Are we at rest, even when things around us are in a state of turmoil? If not, then it's time to fill up.

We have to keep an eye on that expectation gauge. Are we expecting God to work in our life and expecting His promises to come to pass in our future? If not, then it's time to fill up.

How do we fill up? By believing. If we're in doubt, we'll be without. But if we're believing, we'll be receiving!

CHAPTER 5

The Word Is The Key

W e've seen that faith is the starting point for walking
in victory. We've learned that faith produces expectation, expectation produces joy, joy produces strength,
and strength produces victory. That's what we want. That's
the road we want to take.

There's just one problem: Where does faith come from?
The Bible tells us that faith comes from hearing the Word
of God.

ROMANS 10:17
17 *So then faith cometh by hearing, and hearing by
the word of God.*

Faith doesn't come by prayer and fasting. It doesn't come
by having somebody lay hands on us. Faith comes by hearing God's Word.

Now let's go back for a moment and insert the Word of God into the process we've been talking about. The Word produces faith, faith produces expectation, expectation produces joy, joy produces strength, and strength produces victory. We could say, then, that the Word of God is our key to victory. That's our foundation. That's what makes it all work.

If we want victory, then we need to get into the Word and let the Word get into us.

If we're not experiencing much victory in our life, it's because we don't have much of the Word in our life. If we want victory, then we need to get into the Word and let the Word get into us. We need to find a translation of the Bible that we can understand, saturate our mind and our heart with it, and let it lift us to a new level of thinking and believing and living.

How do we raise our level of faith? With the Word. How do we raise our level of expectation? With the Word. How do we raise our level of joy? With the Word. How do we raise our level of strength? With the Word. How do we raise our level of victory? With the Word. The Word is our answer—to everything. We can literally change our world with it.

Psalm 119 is full of statements about the important role the Word of God plays in our victory.

PSALM 119:49-50 (NKJV)

49 Remember the word to Your servant, upon which You have caused me to hope.

50 This is my comfort in my affliction, for Your word has given me life.

PSALM 119:114-116 (NKJV)

114 You are my hiding place and my shield; I hope in Your word.

115 Depart from me, you evildoers, for I will keep the commandments of my God!

116 Uphold me according to Your word, that I may live; and do not let me be ashamed of my hope.

What does David say is the source of his hope and his strength? The Word of God.

Has God given you a word for your family? your finances? your health? your job? your future? If so, do you believe it? If you do, then you'll have confident expectation. All you need is a word from God.

We all face difficulties in this life. Jesus said we would (John 16:33). God doesn't cause our afflictions. Afflictions are just part of living in this world. But David tells us in

Psalm 119 that the Word of God will bring us through our afflictions. The Word of God gives us something on which to base our faith. The Word of God will keep our level of expectation high, even in tough times.

Are you experiencing a tough time right now? If so, what's going to get you through? Expectation. What's going to give you expectation? Faith. And how are you going to get faith? From the Word of God. Faith and expectation come from the Word.

If our expectation is based on God's Word, we won't be disappointed.

David tells us that God holds us up with His Word. That Word produces faith. That faith produces expectation. That expectation produces joy. And that joy produces strength—strength that will carry us all the way through to victory. The Word of God will do that for us.

David goes on to say that our expectations won't end in shame. If our expectation is based on God's Word, we *won't* be disappointed. God *won't* let us down. We *will* see His promises come to pass in our life.

You don't have to be ashamed or embarrassed about trusting in God and believing His Word. If you have even heard *one* word from God, that's enough to give you faith. That's enough to give you expectation. That's enough to give you joy. That's enough to give you strength. That's enough to bring you victory.

Only God is worthy of our trust. If we want to experience victory in life, our faith and expectation must be rooted in Him alone.

PSALM 130:7 (NKJV)

7 O Israel, hope in the LORD; for with the LORD there is mercy, and with Him is abundant redemption.

PSALM 62:5 (NKJV)

5 My soul, wait silently for God alone, for my expectation is from Him.

Is our expectation in events and experiences? Is it centered around people and places? Is it rooted in our work and the world? If so, we're going to be disappointed.

PSALM 62:7-8 (NKJV)

7 In God is my salvation and my glory; the rock of my strength, and my refuge, is in God.

8 Trust in Him at all times, you people; pour out your heart before Him; God is a refuge for us.

Only expectation birthed from a relationship with the Lord Jesus Christ and God's Word will carry us through to victory. We must base our trust in Him at all times.

Do you want to receive the things you're expecting from God? Do you want to see the fulfillment of the promises He has spoken to your heart? The Bible says that you will, if you believe in Him.

ROMANS 9:33 (AMP)

33 *As it is written, Behold I am laying in Zion a Stone that will make men stumble, a Rock that will make them fall; but he who believes in Him [who adheres to, trusts in, and relies on Him] shall not be put to shame nor be disappointed in his expectations.*

If you believe in God—if you adhere to Him, trust in Him, rely on Him—and base your expectations on His Word, you won't be disappointed. You'll be a victor, not a victim.

What kind of world are you living in? Is it a world of disappointment, dread, and discouragement? If so, you can change that today. You can decide to live by choice instead of by chance. You can decide to make a life instead of just a living. You can decide to get ahead instead of just getting by. It all depends on your level of expectation.

If you'll base your expectation on God and His Word, you'll never be defeated again. Bible expectation keeps you going in the toughest of times. Bible expectation energizes you and gives you power in the present to press toward the future. Bible expectation takes obstacles and turns them into opportunities.

Bible expectation is a matter of choice, not chance. God has a future for you—a good future. You want to show up there. You don't want to be shipwrecked. You don't want to be disappointed and ashamed. You want to see His promises come to pass in your life.

So trust Him. Think big. Believe big. Pray big. Expect big. He'll meet you at the level of your expectation!

Additional copies of

The Power of Expectation

are available at fine bookstores everywhere
or directly from:

Church On The Rock
P.O. Box 1668
St. Peters, MO 63376-8668
(314) 240–7775
www.cotr.org

About The Author

Pastor David Blunt and his wife, Kim, are the pastors of Church On The Rock in St. Peters, Missouri. From the days of its small beginning of only 35 people back in 1983, God has had His hand on this ministry. Today, Church On The Rock is a dynamic, growing church of over 4,000 members, with a vision to impact its city and the world with the Gospel of Jesus Christ. This ministry is literally touching the lives of millions of people through the Internet and through the church's weekly national television broadcast, *Principles For Life*.

Pastor Blunt's insights into the Word challenge and inspire believers to grow to new levels in their relationship with God and their service to others. His practical, personable style of teaching causes the Word to come alive in the hearts of people and draws them into a personal encounter with Jesus. This life-changing ministry is committed to raising up and equipping believers to answer the call of God on their lives and to become all that He created them to be.

Also available from David Blunt are the following books:

The Incredible Benefits of Knowing God
God's Benefit: Healing
Wisdom's Winning Ways
The Characteristics of a Plodder
This Life's for You!
How to Get Answers From God

Also available from David Blunt are the following inspirational tape series:

Authority of the Believer
The Key to Triumphant Living
Soaring With Eagles
Take the Limits Off of Your Life

Please send all prayer requests and inquiries to:

Pastor David M. Blunt
Church On The Rock
P.O. Box 1668
St. Peters, MO 63376-8668